"The dream of every parent is t[...] their children build confidence, [...] Steve Gardner's groundbreaking [...] have a fantastic tool to unlock th[...] ...ake those dreams come true! Steve writes wit[...] ...ergy that will engage and captivate both you and your children. *Your Superpowers* is truly transformational—alive with possibility, passion, and inspiration! There is something special in your child just waiting to come out! *Your Superpowers* will help you ignite that magic!"

—Brian Biro, Husband, Father, Speaker,
Author, America's Breakthrough Coach

"I love this book! Get it for your children, grandchildren, nieces, nephews, or any pre-teen or teen you care about, so that they will be able to understand how the universe works. They won't have to go through all the struggles we went through at that age. *Your Superpowers* is going to elevate the world by strengthening and empowering this generation's teenagers. It will strengthen your family, your community, and the planet."

—Dr. Joe Vitale, author The Attractor Factor, mrfire.com

"I loved the book, very well written, young and old should read this. It opened my eyes and brought better energy into my life. I'm now choosing to use my superpowers."

—Kris Denison, Former Miss Utah

YOUR SUPERPOWERS

Volume 1

Dream It, Achieve It

Your Superpowers

Volume 1

Dream It, Achieve It

STEVE GARDNER

Manufactured in the United States of America

10 9 8 7 6 5 4 3 2 1

ISBN: 978-0-9839332-0-5

Library of Congress Cataloging-in-Publication is available

*Dedicated to
my oldest nephew,
Joseph.*

Foreword

Junior high and high school can be a tough few years for anyone. I was no exception. I remember very clearly trying to fit in, trying to make sense of all the changes in life. I didn't discover until years later that those "growing up" years do not have to be all pain and no gain.

If you are a teenager, you know that life can be very unpredictable. You probably know what it feels like to be trapped in lost self-esteem. Almost certainly there are times when you've felt like a big loser. If you have ever questioned what once gave you security or wondered what life is all about, you are normal. But normal is not truly who you are or what you are capable of.

What if I told you that you don't have to feel that way? What if I told you the secret to making sense of it all? If I told you about hidden super-powers within you, would you be interested in unlocking them?

It's all right here: everything you need to become who you really want to be. Read it, apply it, and expect miracles.

Contents

YOUR SUPERPOWERS

Volume 1

Dream It, Achieve It

You Are Greater Than You Realize

You Are Greater
Than You Realize

S top and think for a minute about all of the people you know. Think about your friends, your neighbors, your classmates, and others you see regularly. Out of all of these people, you probably know one or two who really stand out. Every good thing in life just seems to fall into their lap. They are good at sports, they are good at music, and they are popular at school or excel in whatever they pursue. Everyone likes them and wants to be with them. From your perspective, it may feel like they can do no wrong. Everything they do just works out for them. **You may have wondered, "Why did they get all the** good genes? Why are they so blessed? How **do** they do that?"

It may be hard to believe right now, but you have within you the ability to enjoy life just as much as they do. The reason you haven't yet is simple: you don't know how to use your own superpowers. I guess it's not too strange that you haven't—they are, after all, invisible. You probably didn't even know you have them. In this book, I'll help you uncover the secret superpowers that will help you embrace and enjoy your life more completely.

Right now, you have powers greater than anything you have ever imagined. Can you believe that? I'm going to show how you are more powerful than the world's most powerful supercomputer. Not only that, but you are also the world's most powerful and magical magnet. Do you believe me? Whether or not you do, I can prove it to you. Let's start with the supercomputer part.

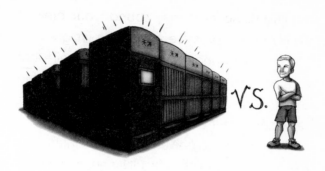

Computers and Brains

Right now, the world's fastest supercomputer is located in China. This marvel is called the Tianhe-1, which means "Milky Way 1" in Chinese. The supercomputer has achieved a computing speed of 2,570 trillion calculations per second. That is 2,570,000,000,000,000 calculations every single second! This supercomputer is not like your dad's computer. It is eight feet tall and fills a large room. Just to operate this machine costs about $20 million each year.

Surprising as it may sound, your brain is even more impressive. Your brain weighs only about three pounds—the size of a softball—but you can learn practically *anything*. The only thing it costs to keep your brain running smoothly is daily food, water, and oxygen.

Your mind is so powerful that as an infant you learned to speak a very difficult language, English, fluently! You learned to recognize shapes, colors, smells, and sounds, and you very quickly began interpreting all this new information.

You started to organize sounds in your mind as they became familiar. Soon those sounds became words that *meant* something to you, and your brain trained your muscles to make those sounds and communicate.

You were a total miracle! You still are! It is too easy to take for granted what an amazing accomplishment it is for an infant with no awareness of language to grow into a 13 year old who not only speaks fluent English but can read and write it, too.

If you have the desire, your brain can learn *any* language. When you hear people speak Chinese, Zulu, or any other languages, the words sound like weird, meaningless babble to you. These crazy, bizarre sounds make just as little sense to you now as English made to you 13 years ago. **Within a couple of years,** however, **your mind can learn any language on this planet.**

No computer can sit for two years and figure out a language. You could play tapes of even the most simple sounds—for example, "mom... dad ... mom" and "water... milk...water"—over and over for five or even ten years and no computer today is "smart" enough to figure out what those words mean.

But *you* learned English, and you can learn Chinese! Isn't that incredible? **If you were a character in Mr. Incredible's family, your super power would be your amazing mind—more powerful than the world's most powerful supercomputer.**

Computers Come from People

About 15 years ago, computers could already do complex math equations very quickly. But they were not nearly as useful as they are today, because they couldn't recognize a human's face, understand a spoken language, or give accurate directions.

Computers can do all of those things very well today. Why are today's computers so much more valuable and better than the computers of 15 years ago? Humans made them that way.

A human, possibly a 13 year old, had an idea of what it would take to "program" a computer to recognize faces. This person figured out a series of mathematical algorithms that allow a computer to measure the distance between someone's eyes, or from the top of the forehead to the nose, or from the length of the jaw line. This human "taught" a computer how to mathematically recognize faces. The same thing happened with voice recognition software, GPS units, and similar advances.

In the future we might have computers that can learn languages easily. For that to happen, another human being will need to teach the computer to associate unknown sounds with new meaning. **Will that person be you?**

Computer-like Brains

Some people have figured out how to use their brains in a way similar to a computer. Laurence Kim Peek, a man from Murray, Utah, was one of those people. When he was still a fetus, his brain developed without a corpus callosum. This body part is located right in the middle of the brain and acts like a bridge so the left and right sides can communicate. Scientists are not sure exactly why, but because Kim Peek's brain

couldn't function like most brains, it created new and unusual connections in order to perform.

Even though Kim did not start to walk until he was four and his IQ was measured as below average, he used his brain in a way that you and I have not yet learned to do. He could memorize what he saw from the age of 16 months!

Kim read books his entire life. It usually took him about an hour to read and memorize each book. He would read both pages at once, using his left eye to read the left page and his right eye to read the right page. **As an adult, he could remember every page of over 12,000 books, including telephone books, dictionaries, and encyclopedias!** How many books do you read each year? Five? 20? 50? If you read 50 books every year, it would take you 240 years to finish 12,000 books!

Brains that
Surpass Computers

Daniel Tammet is another fascinating example of what the brain can do. He can learn languages extremely quickly. One time, he agreed to start learning Icelandic only one week before he appeared on television and conversed in Icelandic with the host.

Altogether, Daniel speaks 10 different languages. He can memorize long numbers—at one competition he recited pi from memory to 22,514 digits. He belives that his mind is not very different from other people's minds.

Other people can listen to difficult songs once, and then play them back on the piano without any mistakes. Still others have learned to master 20 instruments.

Perfect Memory

On December 19, 2010, the television program *60 Minutes* let the world know about very special people who can remember every day of their lives since they were about 10 years old. These people can remember which days it rained or which days it was sunny 30 years ago! They can tell you what they ate for lunch on any given date 18 years ago.

One of these people, Bob Patella, loves sports, and he can tell you about every game played by his favorite teams for the past 30 years. For now, this virtually endless memory is called "superior autobiographical memory." Scientists are just discovering this unique ability, and they are unsure why some people can remember every life occurrence while the rest of us easily forget normal events.

While scientists already understand exactly how a supercomputer works, even after

hundreds of years of studying the brain, there is still more that they *don't* know about the brain than what they do know. That is why Napoleon Hill said, **"Whatever the mind can conceive and believe, it can achieve."**

Unlimited Potential of the Brain

Human brains imagined the idea for computers in the first place, and they continue to this day to use their creativity to make computers smaller, faster, cheaper, and better. Your brain not only has the ability to remember every game you will ever watch, memorize the phone book, and learn to play 20 instruments or speak 10 different languages, it also has the unparalleled ability to create. **That is your real gift: the ability to create** things in your mind and work on them until you have created them physically.

18

I want you to tap your forehead several times and say, "This is the most powerful computer in the world!" How did that feel? Kind of funny? Well, do it again. "This is the most powerful computer in the world!" Now go to your dad, tap his forehead and say, "This is the second most powerful computer in the world!" Ha, just kidding, don't do that. Most people don't like it when someone taps their forehead for no reason.

Unused Superpowers

Sometimes you might feel average or pretty ordinary. That's okay. The feeling isn't an accurate reflection of your abilities. I'm sure the TianHe-1 supercomputer could be used for ordinary things too. The world's fastest computer could add 2 + 2 if that's all its owner wanted it to do. I'm sure it could be used just to play a simple computer game like Tetris or to check email.

Actually, sometimes that is what you do with *your* superpowers. Even though your brain is powerful enough to learn Chinese or know all the rules for every sport in the world, you choose not to. That's right—you *choose* not to, even if you could do it while simultaneously governing your body temperature, breathing, muscle movements, digestion and so much more. You are so powerful and capable a learner that you could come up with your own sport, create your own video game, or even build a boat (perhaps a remote-controlled version). **Your brain is now strong enough to learn *anything*.**

When you feel ordinary, know that it is only because you are choosing not to use all of your superpowers. Instead, you are using your super-computer to add 2 + 2 or check your email.

You Have Superpowers

Now that you realize how powerful your brain is, it's time to learn how to tap into that power.

When I was 13, I thought using my brain meant doing my homework. Ha ha! I was totally wrong. **Now I realize that when I use my brain**

for real, it is *exciting!* It is *fun!* The difference between when I was 13 and now is that I have learned the secrets for using my superpowers. I have unlocked those secrets and want to share them with you.

Make sure, though, that when you learn these secrets, you use them to enrich your environment. Use them wisely to make life more fun for you, your friends, and your family.

YOUR
SECOND
SUPERPOWER

Discovering My Superpower

You have another superpower that you probably don't know about yet. **I had this power when I was nine years old, but I didn't know it yet, either.** At that time I loved to learn about explorers and Native American Indians. I spent hours every day reading books about trailblazers like Daniel Boone and Buffalo Bill Cody. I enjoyed reading or watching documentaries about Crazy Horse, Sitting Bull, and other famous Indians.

I liked the explorer and Indian lifestyle so much that I learned how to do the rain dance and the buffalo dance. I bought some rabbit pelts, and my Grandpa Jim helped me turn one into an explorer's pouch. I learned how to make shelters out of trees and dirt, and I learned how to start a fire without a match or a lighter.

Before long I had made my own Indian drum (yes, I made it myself!). I softened the real leather with a solution and then soaked it so the leather would expand and I could stretch it over a base.

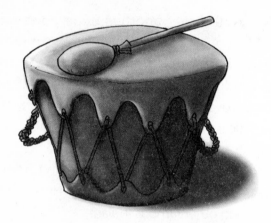

When the leather dried, it hardened so that it made a great sound. I had my own feather head-dress and beads and body armor.

My best friends and I made forts and camped in them. We had a teepee, and many times we would meet together for pow-wows. These in-volved cooking meals over fire and trading our things. We made new pouches and moccasins and arrows and armor with our leather, beads and other supplies.

After I had been heavily involved in this hobby for a couple of years, my mom read in the newspaper about an auction where the police were selling animal pelts to raise money. Early

the morning of the auction, my parents and I arrived filled with eager anticipation. Although the three of us were freezing, the opportunity was worth it. I left that auction with a bobcat fur, two bear pelts (one of them still had the claws in it), beaver pelts and *more*. It was amazing.

I made my own bow out of a tree in our yard (it took me a while to learn which woods were the best for this). I made my own arrows, and I could shoot them so far I could make a field goal

on a football field while standing in the other end zone! I made the bow—*and* the arrows—myself! Before I was 11!

Your Invisible Superpower

You might not care a lot about explorers or Indians from 200 years ago. You do care about some things, though, and when you learn more, you'll discover even *more* things that you will want to explore and do.

Have you ever built your own table? Your own treehouse? Have you ever thought about creating your own dune buggy? Or learning to make crème brûlée? Have you ever had ideas for a new board game or a new sport?

Are you ready to hear about the second superpower you have?

You are not only the world's most powerful

computer, you are also the world's most powerful and magical magnet!

You are probably thinking, "What does a super-magnet have to do with Native American Indians or building a dune buggy?"

Well, it may not be obvious yet, but the answer is **EVERYTHING**!

Invisible Magnetic Power

You have a magnet inside of you. **When you become interested in something,** *anything* at all, then the energy inside of you starts to change.

That energy can magically communicate with other energy all around you. You don't usually feel it happening, but it is *always* happening. **All day, every day, even in your sleep, your energy is communicating with energy all around you.**

That communication goes something like this: when my mind was constantly thinking thoughts like "Indians are so *cool*, I *love* learning more about Indians," my energy changed so that I started attracting, just like a magical magnet, books and videos about Indians. I really enjoyed that, and so I kept attracting more and more cool Indian things to me. I had more and more fun.

Because I enjoyed what I was doing, when I had a new idea, things came together. For example, when I wanted to make a pouch out of a rabbit pelt, my grandfather magically came to visit for the first time in 30 years. He had both the time and the skills needed to make a really cool pouch with me.

My mother knew of my interest in pelts, and

because my energy was communicating with her energy, her eyes were drawn to the newspaper ad about the police auction. Because we woke up early and traveled to an auction in the freezing cold, we were able to buy animal skins for very little money even though they would normally have cost a small fortune. In other words, my energy and excitement at that time *attracted* those things to me.

Using Your Invisible Magnet

Because I am a powerful magnet, I attracted all those opportunities into my life. Because it was so fun and exciting for me to learn and grow, **I *acted* every time I had a good opportunity.**

I didn't know this when I was your age, but I was *attracting* all of that fun and excitement into my life.

You are doing the same thing now. Without even realizing it, your energy is constantly communicating with the energy all around you. The things that you think about and the feelings you feel create your energy, and *everything* in your life is there because your super-magnet helped bring it there.

Stop and think about that. Everything you are experiencing is something you helped attract to yourself.

Action Is Necessary

I s there something you would like to attract into your life? Is there something in your life now that you didn't want to attract?

The good news is that you can have control over your life *if* you choose to. Most 13 year olds just choose to use their superpowers to do ordinary things, like add 2 + 2. Instead, they could be using their superpowers to learn new languages, create new games, truly enjoy life, and reach unbelievable goals!

So, what are the steps to taking control of your life? I really wish someone would have shared them with me when I was your age. Here are the secrets to using your superpowers.

GETTING STARTED

Secret Superpower
Step #1

Become Aware

Become aware of yourself. Become aware of your thoughts. Are you happy? When are you happiest? When are you not happy? What makes you frustrated? What makes you sad?

When I was 13, three things always seemed to frustrate me. The most common? Homework and teachers. I had some pretty cool teachers, but for the most part I was always frustrated in school. My teachers said that my handwriting was too sloppy, that I was too loud in class, and that I didn't get my homework done.

At that time I just let it frustrate me. I didn't realize then that my teachers had forgotten to tell me how creative I was, how cool it was that I had learned about history all by myself, or how admirable it was that I could play basketball non-stop for four hours a day without getting tired or bored.

School Struggles

Your teachers, if they are like mine used to be, probably manage to make school frustrating for you, too. It is so easy for them to worry about rules, deadlines and homework and forget the incredible things you can build, that you know the latest sports scores, or that you are surprisingly creative.

In addition to school being one of my most constant frustrations, I was also regularly frustrated by mean classmates and having a weird family.

Bullies

Sometimes other kids at school would do mean things just to be mean. **Some people thought that if they were mean enough, they could prove that they were cool.** Kids today can be just like that.

What's really happening is that their energy is so low they believe they can only be cool if they make fun of others. They are wrong, but because that is what they believe, their energy will continue to attract more opportunities to be mean.

What bullies don't realize is that when they are mean to others, their energy attracts mean people to them, too. When they make fun of other kids, their energy opens the door to people who will make fun of them. I feel sorry for these bullies and you can, too. Sometimes just a few acts of kindness can help them see their bad judgment, and they can change their energy pretty quickly when they want to.

Family

My third frustration was my weird family. I sometimes felt like my parents were there just to torture me. I disliked piano lessons, and they forced me to take them. I didn't like school, and it made me feel frustrated when my parents checked up on my schoolwork.

At that time, I simply wasn't aware that I was a magnet and actually bringing these frustrations to myself. I didn't know that my thoughts and feelings created my energy, and that my energy was always communicating with other energy in the universe and bringing more of what I thought about back to me. **I've since learned that I must monitor my "inside world" so that I could influence my "outside world."**

So, the first secret step to using your superpowers is to become aware of your thoughts and feelings.

Understanding Your Feelings

Before you read on, take out a pen or pencil and write down three things that make you truly happy.

1 _____

_____

2 _____

_____

3 _____

_____

Next, write down three things that frustrate you or make you sad.

1 _____

_____

2 _____

_____

3 _____

_____

Now take time to think. Why do those things frustrate you? Why do the happy things make you happy? **Before you can go on to the second secret step, you must be aware of your thoughts and feelings.**

As soon as you know what you enjoy and also what frustrates you, you can move on to the next chapter.

BEGINNING THE CHANGE

Secret Superpower
Step #2

Set Your Intentions

The second secret step to using your super-powers is to set your intentions. By choosing to believe your new intentions, you change your energy so that instead of attracting bad things to you, you attract happiness.

Setting intentions is something you've done many times before but have never realized. These intentions are what you want to attract. From step one you already know what you want and don't want. **Now it's your turn to start changing your energy so you attract the best in life back to you.**

Look at what you wrote down for your frustrations. Now, what conditions would need to change for those frustrations to be moved to the fun list? For me, my number-one frustration was

"School is boring and feels long and difficult."

To change that, in step two I would write:

"School is fun, feels short, and is easy."

Or, if I wrote in step one
"My teachers don't like me."
I could change my intention to be:
"My teachers all like me and encourage me."

A frustration like *"Homework is boring and stupid."* Would need an intention like *"My homework is fun and useful."*

For mean schoolmates, the frustration that says

"Kids at school are mean to me."

Would become

"Kids at school are nice to me, and even when someone tries to be mean, it doesn't make me feel bad because I know that the bully/mean kid just has bad energy, and probably has a lot of people who are mean to him/her. I feel pity for them and wish them well."

My frustration of

"My parents are weird and always try to make my life difficult."

Would need an intention like

"My parents are cool and always try to make my life more enjoyable."

So take some time now to write out your intentions.

1 _____

_____

2 _____

_____

3 _____

_____

4 _____

_____

5 _____

_____

6 _____

_____

7 _____

_____

8 _____

_____

The Power of Writing
Down Your Intentions

Why do you need to write down these intentions? Remember that your beliefs, thoughts, and feelings create your energy. Your energy acts like a magnet to bring more of these things to you.

If you believe that your parents' main job is to make life difficult for you, then your energy will communicate with their energy. You will inadvertently bring back to you, like an invisible magnet, more things that will make you feel like your parents are out to get you. The same thing happens with teachers and mean kids at school or anything else.

It may be hard to believe, but some of your classmates *enjoy* school! Why is that? It's because of their superpowers. Because they believe that school is fun, their energy goes out and attracts back to them, just like a magnet, all the fun and positive things about school.

You can do that, too, with *everything* you find frustrating right now. **You can use your superpower to attract good and fun things back to you, instead of the boring, mean, or frustrating things.**

Envision the Change

Take a few minutes right now to imagine what it will *feel* like when your intentions become true. Imagine your teacher telling you how proud she is of you, and how happy you are that you can spell every word on your spelling homework. See yourself playing the piano *really* well and *loving* it!

Imagine all the people complimenting you when you finish playing a beautiful song on the piano. How does it feel to score the winning goal in your soccer game? Can you see all of your new friends? How do you feel now that school is a fun place for you? How does it feel to *want* to go to school?

Doesn't that feel wonderful!!!?!!

As your energy changes, your new reality is taking form.

So far so good, right? Not too difficult. It is becoming exciting to realize that you have these powers. Now you are ready to move on to the next chapter.

THE ULTIMATE ALLIANCE

Secret Superpower
Step #3

Let Heavenly Father Help You

Whatever your religious background, you likely realize there is a life force or a source of all energy. You can call this greater power God or the divine. Some people call it the universe. In this book, I refer to this power as Heavenly Father.

How do you let Heavenly Father help you? He has taught us that if we ask for something, He will give it to us. **One way He helps us is by helping us change our energy so that we can attract new, better things to us.**

If we pray and ask Heavenly Father to make school easier, take away the bullies in school, or change our parents, He of course will want to say to us, "I gave you *two* superpowers, not just one. You have the world's most powerful supercomputer, *and* your energy magically and magnetically communicates with the energy all around you to attract your experiences to you. If I gave you those superpowers, do you think I want you to figure out how to use them? *Of course* I do!"

Communicating with the Divine

So how do you communicate with God? It's easier than you might think. You have divinity inside of you. Because of that, you can communicate with, and receive help from, your Heavenly Father. To begin, find a calm, peaceful place where you can be by yourself for a while.

Think about a few things that make you truly happy. Just sit for a minute and enjoy those wonderful thoughts.

When the time feels right, begin to address the divine. When I do this, I simply say "Dear Heavenly Father." When you say or think those words in this state of peace and gratitude, you have begun to pray.

You can talk to Heavenly Father just like you would talk to a good friend. Tell Him what is making you happy. Thank Him for all the things that come to your mind.

Then, think about the intentions you wrote. With that same tender feeling of gratitude, tell Heavenly Father that you are changing your energy so that each of your intentions is becoming true for you. Thank Heavenly Father for helping you change your energy, and for bringing joy to you.

You can know, just as sure as the sun will rise again tomorrow morning, that Heavenly Father is helping you, so be sure to thank Him and be aware of His help.

Because of the way I understand my relationship with the divine, I finish each of my prayers with Him by saying "in the name of Jesus Christ, amen." If you don't already have a preferred method for communicating with Heavenly Father, you can do the same.

Isn't that easy? It may seem really strange at first. As you are doing it, though, you will feel the divinity inside of you. You will feel warm, peaceful, and happy. When you experience those feelings, you'll know that true communication is

happening. Continue to use prayer regularly to make sure your energy is where you want it to be.

Great Tool for Improvement

When you pray, don't ask Heavenly Father to change your parents. Instead, ask Him to help you change your energy so you attract the fun, exciting things of school back to you, rather than the bad, boring or difficult things.

Similarly, don't ask Him to change your teachers or your school. Instead, ask Him to help you change your energy so you attract the fun, exciting things of school back to you, instead of the bad, boring or difficult things.

When you have a bad day, you know it is because your energy brought those bad things to you. You know that you need to change your energy.

Heavenly Father is really happy when His children figure this out. He is so happy and willing to help you change your energy, because that is when you are using the superpowers He gave you to improve your life. The cool thing is, because you are using the tools you were given to solve problems, **you will find that the problems are solved much faster than ever before**.

Heavenly Father will help you change your energy so that you attract different people and different experiences into your life. Even though it may seem impossible for school to be fun or cool right now, you can find students in your classes and at other schools who enjoy what they are learning. If your energy changes, you can start to enjoy school, too.

True Change, Real Improvement

If your energy allows it, your parents will seem like the kindest, coolest people in the whole world! (This is because *your* energy is communicating with their energy and is bringing out the coolness in them so you can enjoy it.)

Almost as if by magic, your school, your friends, your family, your sports—everything will seem to go better for you. Life will just magically improve, and you will start to enjoy learning and growing and just being *you.*

When your energy is not good, your teachers seem too strict, your classmates are mean, schoolwork is boring or stupid, and your mom and dad are annoying.

So if you want things to change, be sure to use your superpowers and let Heavenly Father help!

ACTION!

Secret Superpower

Step #4

Listen for Promptings

Now that you are aware of what you do and don't want, have set intentions to change your energy and asked for divine help, you are going to feel prompted to do or say things, different things. It is impossible to know ahead of time what you will be inspired to do or say, but because you are changing your energy and have asked for help, you will receive help in the form of promptings.

A prompting may tell you to do something as small as to smile. It may be to start reading a certain book or to talk to a teacher. **Whatever the prompting is, your job is to *hear* it and *do* it.**

Even when what you feel prompted to do doesn't make any sense, you must still follow it. Your job is to act. Beware of a common trap: when many people feel like the prompting doesn't make any sense or is too simple to do any good, they will dismiss the prompting and ignore it. You can never let yourself fall into that trap. Always follow those promptings, even when you don't know why.

Stay with It

I have to warn you here: if you haven't been using your superpowers your whole life and suddenly start changing your energy and attracting happiness and fun, it might seem, well, different. That is, until you get the hang of it.

But even if it feels weird, you have to *do* what you are prompted to do. Remember that your energy is attracting really cool things to you, but if you don't recognize them, they won't make you happier. If you ignore the new things that are attracted to you, then your energy just changes back to what it used to be.

Many times you will be prompted to do things that you have done before. As you do them, you'll find that because your energy is different, the thing that you are doing (babysitting, piano, or homework, for example) *feels* different. It isn't as boring or dumb as it used to be. If you continue to let your energy change, then the activity that used to be stupid can become fun and even cool.

Of course, it always seems easier to just stay where you are and have the same old boring, bad life. It seems easier because you don't have to change your energy, you don't have to listen for promptings, and you don't have to act on the promptings. Life like this might be boring and frustrating, but at least it seems easy.

Acting on the promptings should feel like a big game. **You can approach each prompting with a playful curiosity.** "I wonder what I am going to learn as I complete this task," or "I wonder where this is going to lead me." Your attitude should be one of joy and wonder, because deep down you expect that each prompting is taking you one step closer to manifesting your intention. How exciting!

Real Growth

The truth is that the only reason it seems easier is because you haven't started using your superpowers yet. You are doing something new.

Once you get the hang of things and it is easy to use your superpowers, you'll look back and think how silly it was that at one time you didn't manage or control your energy. **For the rest of your life, you will probably look around at all the people not using their superpowers and wonder what they are afraid of.** You will discover that either they don't know they have superpowers or they just don't want to dust them off and use them.

If only they knew these secret steps, because life is so much easier and more fun when you use your superpowers!

THE POWER OF GRATITUDE

Secret Superpower
Step #5

Be Grateful for the Improvements

Now that you have learned how to improve your life, school is becoming more fun, your parents seem to trust you, and life is just plain awesome, it is time to take a minute and be grateful for what has happened.

Take a deep breath, all the way in… Fill your lungs as full as they can go, and then slowly let all the air out.

Together, with Heavenly Father, you have created a better life. Way to go! Now it's time to take a few minutes to write down everything that is changing or improving for you as a result of uncovering and using your superpowers.

The first time you read this book, you are just discovering these powers and how to use them. **But every day from now on, you need to take a few minutes to think about the changes in your life and write down the things that make**

you grateful. Use these spaces to keep track of how you use your superpowers.

_____

_____

_____

_____

_____

_____

_____

_____

_____

_____

_____

_____

_____

_____

_____

_____

_____

_____

_____

_____

_____

_____

_____

_____

_____

_____

_____

_____

_____

_____

_____

_____

_____

_____

_____

_____

_____

_____

_____

_____

_____

_____

_____

_____

_____

_____

_____

_____

_____

_____

_____

_____

_____

_____

_____

_____

_____

_____

_____

_____

_____

_____

_____

_____

_____

_____

_____

_____

_____

Take a few minutes to pray and thank Heavenly Father for His help, and for giving you these abilities in the first place.

Gratitude Helps You

Recognizing your blessings and feeling grateful for them is not only the right thing to do, it actually helps you, too. When you feel *sincere* gratitude in your heart, you improve your energy level and actually attract more joyful things back to you. As you feel gratitude for this new batch of blessings, you improve your energy level once more and the cycle continues. It is a wonderful cycle to be in.

Taking Your Superpowers to the Next Level

Now that you understand how to use your superpowers, you are ready to take them to the next level. You can expand and use them to make life even better! You don't have to use your energy only to fix problems. You can also set intentions to improve on things that are going well.

Think about all the places you would like to go, all the things you would like to do, all the

4. Fly an airplane

5. Start my own Successful Business

6. Walk on the Great Wall of China

7. Read 5 Books a year.

8. Lean a New Language

9. Finish School

10. Be on Television

11. Become Great at Basketball

12. Visit the Pyramids

cool things you could make, and all the fun you could have, just as long as your energy is where you want it to be.

I have a list of 50 things that I am working on now. These are things that I want to do before I die. Now it is your turn to make your own list. Write down 50 things, big and small, that you would like to do before you die. Some may be things you can do right now; for others, you may need to spend years to accomplish them. On my list I have fun things like "fly an airplane" and "start my own successful business." I also have easier things like "walk on the Great Wall of China."

I made my first list of 50 things to do before I die about 13 years ago, and I'm almost finished with it. Because I had finished so many of the things on my list, about six years ago I made a second list. I have now finished my third list of 50 things to do before I die, and it is fun to work on learning new things, going to new places, and crossing things off of my list. Most recently I crossed off "ride an elephant in Thailand."

Use the spaces below to fill in *your* list of 50 things to do before you die.

1 _____

2 _____

3 _____

4 _____

5 _____

6 _____

7 _____

8 _____

9 _____

10 _____

11 _____

12 _____

13 _____

14 _____

15 _____

16 _____

17 _____

18 _____

19 _____

20 _____

21 _____

22 _____

23 _____

24 _____

25 _____

26 _____

27 _____

28 _____

29 _____

30 _____

31 _____

32 _____

33 _____

44 _____

35 _____

36 _____

37 _____

38 _____

39 _____

40 _____

41 _____

42 _____

43 _____

44 _____

45 _____

46 _____

47 _____

48 _____

49 _____

50 _____

You Are a Creator!

Now that you have your list, you have a list of 50 intentions. Ask for Heavenly Father's help to accomplish those things, and always remember to be grateful for the things you accomplish. Turn your list into a bookmark so you can see it every day. **You are a creator! You are awesome, and your superpowers will become more and more powerful over time as you learn to use them.**

You came to this earth to learn how to make it a better place. Now that you understand your superpowers, you will find no limit to the great things you can do.

Choose to live right, to be happy and grateful, and expect miracles!

Notes

Notes

Notes

Notes

Steve Gardner as a keynote speaker has spoken in Europe and Asia, in addition to the United States. Steve has been interviewed on talk shows in China and Romania and is a popular speaker in the United States as well. (Steve is fluent in both Romanian and Mandarin Chinese) Steve speaks to youth, young adults, and adults about empowerment. He mixes humor with powerful stories to inspire and teach audiences wherever he goes. If you would like to contact Steve to speak to your group visit his website at DiscoveringLifeNow.com.

Additional copies of *Your Superpowers: Dream It, Achieve It* are also available at DiscoveringLifeNow.com in audio, electronic and paperback versions.

Come back regularly to be the first to order volume two, coming soon!

DiscoveringLifeNow.com